A little Book for A little Cook

COPYRIGHT 1905
BY L. P. HUBBARD.

PUBLISHED BY
Pillsbury, Minneapolis

DIRECTIONS

1. Always use Pillsbury's Best Flour.

2. Sift flour twice before adding to cakes or breakfast cakes.

3. Make all measurements level by using edge of knife to lightly scrape off from top of cup or spoon until material is even with the edges.

4. Use same sized cups or spoons in measuring for the same recipe.

5. Before starting to make recipe, read through carefully, then put on table all the materials and tools needed in making that particular recipe.

A NOTE TO THE MODERN READER

A Little Book for a Little Cook was originally published by Pillsbury in 1905. This new reproduction has all of the recipes from the original softcover edition, but is being reissued with the modern reader in mind. The collector will note some small departures from the original book, but the little cook will no doubt find what is here to be fun to cook, delicious, and warmly nostalgic.

For best results, we recommend the following recipe changes when preparing these old-fashioned recipes. When using Pillsbury BEST® Flour, there is no need to sift the flour. Just lightly spoon the flour into the measuring cup and level it off. When combining the flour with other dry ingredients, stir the ingredients together with a fork.

Bread: Soak 1 (.6 oz.) cake compressed yeast or 1 pkg. active dry yeast and 1 tablespoon sugar in 2 tablespoons lukewarm (105-110°F.) water for 2 minutes. Knead dough 5 to 10 minutes. Let dough rise in warm place until it is <u>almost double in size</u>. Grease, bottom only, 8x4 or 9x5-inch loaf pan. Bake at 375°F. for 35 to 40 minutes or until light golden brown.

Biscuits: Bake on a lightly greased cookie sheet at 425°F. for 9 to 11 minutes.

Ginger Bread: Bake in a greased 13x9-inch pan at 350°F. for 23 to 27 minutes.

Sponge Cake: Bake in a greased and floured 9-inch square or 11x 7- inch pan at 350°F. for 24 to 29 minutes.

Muffins: Bake in a greased 12-cup muffin pan at 400°F. for 12 to 16 minutes.

Creamed Potatoes: If a double boiler is unavailable, cook in a heavy saucepan over medium heat until mixture thickens, about 5 minutes.

Fudge: Cook in a small heavy saucepan; pour mixture into a buttered 9x5 or 8x4-inch pan.

Chocolate Cake: Bake in a greased and floured 8-inch square pan at 350°F. for 23 to 27 minutes or until toothpick inserted in center comes out clean.

Johnny Cake: Bake in a greased 8-inch square pan at 400°F. for 15 to 20 minutes.

BREAD

MATERIAL:

½ cup boiling water   2 tablespoons cold water
½ cup milk   1 teaspoon salt
½ cake yeast   3 cups Pillsbury's Best

WAY OF PREPARING:

Soak yeast in 2 tablespoons cold water. Pour ½ cup boiling water into ½ cup milk. <u>Let cool to luke warm.</u> Stir in dissolved yeast and salt. Add 3 cups Pillsbury's Best. Turn onto a kneading board. Knead until smooth. Let rise until three times the original size. Knead slightly, put into a well greased pan. Let rise until double its bulk and bake 25 or 30 minutes in moderate oven. It will be well to consult some experienced person as to lightness of sponge and dough.

BISCUITS

MATERIAL:

1 cup Pillsbury's Best
½ teaspoon salt
2 teaspoons baking powder
1 tablespoon cold butter
½ cup milk

WAY OF PREPARING:

Sift flour, salt and baking powder twice. Chop butter in with a knife until mealy. Add milk for a soft dough. Place on a board with a little flour. Knead gently until smooth. Roll out to one-half inch thickness. Use small cutter and place biscuits in greased pan. Bake in a hot oven until nicely browned.

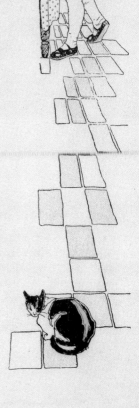

GINGER BREAD

MATERIAL:

½ cup molasses
1 cup sugar
5 tablespoons melted
butter
½ teaspoon cinnamon
½ teaspoon ginger

1 teaspoon salt
1 teaspoon soda
1 egg
2½ cups
Pillsbury's Best
1 cup hot water

WAY OF PREPARING:

Put molasses in a bowl. Add sugar, melted butter, cinnamon and ginger. Put soda and salt in a cup and fill with hot water. Stir into first mixture. Add flour, then well beaten egg. Beat hard. Bake for thirty minutes in a well greased pan. Watch oven closely, as ginger bread burns easily. This makes a good sized cake.

"Here are Felix and
Mary Ann
Looking in at the
Gingerbread Man,
Which was baked in
the baker's pan;
Cloves for his eyes and
paste for his tie,—
Wondering whether
the price is high."

SPONGE CAKE

MATERIAL:

1 cup sugar
2 eggs
½ cup hot water
1¼ cups Pillsbury's Best
1½ teaspoons baking powder
pinch of salt
½ teaspoon vanilla

WAY OF PREPARING:

Separate eggs, beating whites to a stiff froth. Set them aside. Beat yolks until thick. Add sugar gradually, then water, salt, flour and baking powder. Beat thoroughly. Fold in whites and add vanilla. Bake twenty minutes in a buttered and floured shallow pan in moderate oven.

MUFFINS

MATERIAL:

⅓ cup butter
¼ cup sugar
¼ teaspoon salt
1 egg
2 cups Pillsbury's Best
4 teaspoons baking powder
1 cup milk

WAY OF PREPARING:

Beat butter, sugar and egg until creamy. Add milk little at a time, stirring in gradually flour sifted with salt and baking powder. Grease muffin pan, heat slightly, put in mixture and bake in quick oven.

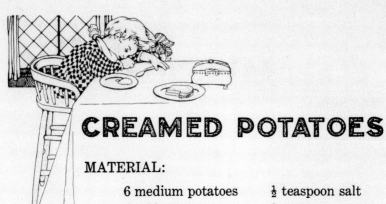

CREAMED POTATOES

MATERIAL:

6 medium potatoes	½ teaspoon salt
3 tablespoons	⅛ teaspoon pepper
Pillsbury's Best	1½ cups milk
2 tablespoons butter	

WAY OF PREPARING:

Pare potatoes, cut into dice, wash in cold water. Cover with boiling water, salt and place on range. Boil until tender, but not mealy. Have ready the cream dressing. This is made by rubbing flour and butter together, adding the milk, salt and pepper, and cooking in double boiler, stirring constantly until like custard. Drain potatoes of water, let them steam a moment, then stir lightly into dressing. Serve hot.

FUDGE

MATERIAL:

1½ tablespoons butter   2 tablespoons
1 cup sugar   molasses
¼ cup milk   1 square chocolate
          ½ teaspoon vanilla

WAY OF PREPARING:

Melt butter in a granite pan. Add sugar, milk and molasses, stirring gently until sugar is dissolved. Boil slowly without stirring for five minutes. Add chocolate square and stir until melted. Boil again until a little of mixture dropped in cold water seems brittle. Take from range, add vanilla, beat until it begins to thicken, then pour into a buttered pan. Cool and mark into squares.

JOHNNY CAKE

MATERIAL:

¾ cup corn meal

¾ cup Pillsbury's Best

3 teaspoons baking powder

½ teaspoon salt

2 tablespoons sugar

1 egg

1 cup milk

1 tablespoon melted butter

WAY OF PREPARING:

Sift cornmeal, flour, baking powder, sugar and salt together. Add milk gradually, well beaten egg and melted butter. Grease shallow pan, heat slightly, pour in mixture and bake twenty minutes in hot oven.

LITTLE TALKS
WITH LITTLE COOKS

The table around which the household gathers three times a day furnishes the chief opportunity for showing the results of good training, whether received in school or home. We show our unselfishness in preferring one another, anticipating one another's wants.

On the table is shown the result of the unselfish thought and care of the chief home-maker. The labor connected with the preparation of the meal is either a burden or a pleasure as one's previous training has made possible.

We get the best training for active life, in other than household work, early in life, at school and home. Why not learn to be good home-makers while still young?

We like to do what we do well. If we learn early, we learn easily and well—the work is a pleasure and success is assured.

Beginners should master the little recipes included in this book. They require only a small amount of material, but enough for success.

THIS is the tale that was told to me

By a loaf of home-made bread, you see,

As it sat one night on the pantry shelf—

A loaf on each side of it—just like itself,

While grouped around stood the pies and cakes,

The good old kind like mother makes,

And one and all then and there confessed

That they owed their existence to Pillsbury's Best.

I SEEM to trace through the distant haze

   My byegone life in the good old days;

     I see in my vision a field of wheat—

     I knew I was there that the world might eat—

I drank of the showers and the morning dew;

In the noonday sun I throve and grew—

     Grew on the verge of a sunny crest,

     Just as fast as I could for Pillsbury's Best.

AND when I had grown both tall and strong

The reapers came—a merry throng—

And through the fields they wend their way,

Just to and fro through the livelong day.

Perhaps they were rude—for they cut me dead—

But what if they did?—I kept my head

And turned on my back and laughed in glee

At the thought of the good, good flour I'd be.

I KNOW I was good, yet the day came at last

When they said I'd be better if soundly thrashed.

Please pardon me here — I can't dwell on this much,

The subject is painful — my feelings are such.

Oh my! but the straw, it flew high in the air

And the chaff chaffed unceasing, but I didn't care,

My laughter rang forth with increased vim and zest,

My chastisement I knew — just meant Pillsbury's Best.

A ND then came the time when I journeyed away
　　To the mills where the "Roller Mills" roll all day,
　And all of them smiled with a happy grin
　And welcomed us poor little wheatlets in;
Oh! the grind of life — I was grasped and seized,
I really can't say I was very much pleased;
　　But to say the least, I was much impressed,
　　And when I got through I was Pillsbury's Best.

The mills where the roller mills
roll all day.

AND now in the latest fashions gay

In the big round world I have my say,

For in this most becoming sack,

Please note the hang — both front and back,

I journey far from the land of my birth

To feed the hungry hordes of Earth;

For those who know ne'er fail to say

That Pillsbury's flour o'er the world holds sway.

TO the kitchen I go — to the bakers who bake
    The bread and the cookies, the pies and the cake;
  It was there that I met the package of yeast
  Who raised the dough for the coming feast,
And that's why I sit and talk to-night,
For to-morrow I know I'll be out of sight;
    So I'll toast myself ere this tale I close,
    To Pillsbury's Best, the flour one knows.

This is the tale of the loaf on the shelf.
As told to me by the loaf itself.